THOSE WHO SPEAK CROW

Poems by

Wayne F. Burke

Dedicated to the crows, sparrows, black-birds, blue-jays, robins, grosbeaks, cardinals, woodpeckers, pigeons, hawks, seagulls, eagles, turkeys, squirrels, chipmunks, woodchucks, muskrats, beavers, raccoons, fish, fox, moose, deer, skunks, and all other creatures of the landscape who inhabit these poems by name or spirit.

Contents

4 PM

Gray and
damp,
a river of crows
flow overhead to
distant tree tops,
a ruckus of
crow shouts—
what is the
racket all about
I wonder.

Pigeons circle rooftops as
the sun sets
and the ridge line
darkens, and
the red brick buildings
turn brown,
and store windows black,
and thousands of crows
flow
like a river of
scraps through the
purple-tinged sky
and I wonder why
they do that
each November,
don't you?

Melt

crystal streams of water
on sidewalks
of glass

brown leaf scabbers
across a mile of parking lot
to greet me

roadside snow chunks
of March
sculpted by
Arp
Brancusi

Misty Mountain
wears a shroud—
the ridge line weeps

Morning #2

a misty morning and
rain-slick streets;
2 crows flapping through
gray soup du jour, and
birds twittering from
somewhere,
maybe under eaves, or
under what tree leaves
remain on branches
mostly bare…Cold air
before snow fall.

8 AM

I got up and out
of the bed
of wrinkled promises
and walked to the window
and looked out at the gray mist
and 3 grosbeaks on a tree
limb
then 5
now 6
little door knockers,
smoke from chimneys drifts
across black roofs
trees like shadows
in the mist—
distant Misty Mountain
yet
to exist.

Smoke

chimneys cooking
houses smoking
a jet pierces the blue sky
like a needle—
the chimneys go through
two packs
by
noon
and still
pouring smoke
dissipating into
washed-out blue
infinitude of
glass ceiling
the sun glares
through.

Marriage

mica flecks of snow
in sunshine
and wind-blown snow spray
of confetti
at the marriage of
Mountain and
Sky
her gossamer lady
white-veiled, shining
beaming a smile on the
ridge line crowd
standing shoulder to shoulder
"do you UUUUU," says the
wind—
"I do ouuuuuu," says the
Sky—
Mountain, imperturbable and
balding, is
silent
because
mountains do not speak
except
when falling.

January in Vermont

sun out today—
a fake one
but
better than none;
I turn my face up
to the light
and pretend
it is June,
flowers in bloom,
green leaves
green hillsides;
I sit on the
grass, sun tan lotion on
my skin
oh yass
nothing quite like
summertime
in Vermont.

Late September afternoon and

the sun fading
fast, only a husk
of what it was
a month ago;
an ambulance sings a siren
song, to the
rescue
but not of
the sinking sun, done
for, tepid
pale
dim-bulb
could not melt
wax, but
still good for
a sunset,
orange & red.

Gray Sky

Black birds in a swarm above
tree leaves turned orange:
shredded sky of clouds
the sun sinks behind
and dies
as a gray snapping turtle
ridden by a frog, moves-in
and swallows
sun
then sky, which survives
in a small blue window
that opens for the
sun
to glide through,
then the frog,
then the turtle,
both of whom
disappear in the
new
blue all-over.

Leaf Peepers

the camera-carrying people are back:
they are taking pictures of the leaves
the trees
the church steeples
the park statues—
snap-happy people
from somewhere else;
people who have no name;
some who speak in a strange dialect,
some who don't;
they stop to gawk,
take a snap-shot
and walk on
to the next view—
people a lot like me and you
but not quite:
they are peepers
and they live in
different time zones
different zip codes.

Whistle

the train whistle
blows a loud
hello
a soft
so long
a clarion
call
up
&
down
the
line.

Clank Clank

here comes the train
with a whistle and
double engines, then
clang clang clang
of boxcars hammering
the trestle, rusted, old, and
groaning; sciatica and shingles
deaf in one ear and arthritic, but
still strong
enough.

Late Fall

got the woolen hat out of the
closet and onto my head because
a cold rain falls on the
yellow, orange, and red leaves.

the muddy river roars to the
junction of another morning of
mist and fog, ruled by minor
and inhospitable gods.

the sun peeks through
a charcoal cloud and
turns to gold
yellow leaves atop black boughs.

distant ridge line of rusty-
orange, lemon-yellow, and
mauve, with pewter-glow of
undergrowth—patches of pine.

spider arms of trees, denuded;
need to find my gloves and
scarf, walk among fallen leaves
blushing red, burnished brown.

drooping heads of sunflowers
bowing
to the inevitable

an old crow welcomes me
to the parking lot
of the nursing home

Sirens

going off
in the city
have nothing to do
with me;
not much does
lately;
not the phone calls I get
and delete,
uninterested in what
they are selling,
and the messages
they are leaving;
not interested in much
at all
lately
here
on Planet Crouton.

Above the MOBIL Station

an angel in the sky
wings spread,
a Michelangelo-beard
and snowy robe
with billowing folds,
followed by a plesiosaur,
tail above the ridge line
of pines
standing shoulder to shoulder
like a watching crowd,
one big knotty
Indian Chief
with headdress
standing alone—
he who gives the order
to the rest
to start downhill,
overrun the town.

Late Summer Day

of bright sunshine and
cool breeze, vanilla
clouds floating over a frolic
of trees; poplar leaves
shining like silver dollars
and the parking lot
dreaming
asphalt dreams.

Meditation

nine minutes into my daily
meditation and
a tapping at the door,
a maid
slim brown woman
frizzy hair tied
back
I tell her she can skip my room;
her affect flat,
can not read it;
I ask if she will lose money
if I refuse,
"no."
Alright then
I close the door,
my mediation over
my emptied mind ready
or not
for samsara world.

Dud

great wall of China cloud
the sun sinks into
bright eye
closing;
last tee-peed rays
spread on a choppy ocean
of divots:
blue-gray air craft carrier on
horizon
sails away—
a dud sunset,
except for aftermath
of gray natural bridge
and hot orange flame
plus purple waves
coming to shore like
a synchronized swim.

Puddles

deep as Lake Tanganyika
full of tree branches, telephone wires, clouds
and sky
endless and
unfathomable,
even by
Hubble.

Sultry

an orange moon
in a dusky sky
on a sultry night:
a chorus of peepers peeping
"so what! so what!"
Outline of the great pine
and ridge line
and sound of traffic sweeping-up;
crickets pick-up the cadence,
lower trill, higher tweet
of mambo from the
hedge row;
a roach clacking castanets,
a conga line of Lady Bugs
and Jimminy Crickets beneath
roses who nod their heads
as the moon flashes yellow
blue, and red
like a strobe light.

Backyard

I want a private spot
to sit
and read
and write
or
take a nap,
feed the birds,
keep a cat,
play in the dirt
if I want to:
study the shadows
the sunlight makes;
a little table
to put my coffee cup on,
a view of sky
and quiet time,
all I can get,
that's it.

The croaking crows;
their black flight into
shadow, into
shade—
what do they croak about
anyway?
I'd like to know,
but can't, because
do not speak crow.

Murmur of the
          river
               high, rolling
                    gold & green
               white froth
          ripples
        squiggles
     wiggles
          downstream
                    under the bridge
               old & gray
            and
       around
          the bend
                under the old
                     rusted trestle
               still able to
          bear the
        weight of
          the choo-
                choo
                    train.

Dogfight

I wonder at the great squawk
made by crows
flying the tree-tops,
until a hawk
flies from shadow
chased by a crow, like
a bi-plane against a B-52
hard to say who
is chasing whom, the
hawk moves in big arcs
the crow
a straighter path
both in blue sky
silent
after the hawk
flies
off.

Sunday

The hiss of leaves, wind-
blown,
a cold November breeze
across an empty city street,
Sunday afternoon. Skittering, crackly
crinkled paper dry and
browned,
air-born now: like the
pigeons,
looking like little crosses,
swirling
around the church steeple.

Void

cloud personages passing in review
before the disc
of the nearly immovable sun
a white thing
burning
since the world began
4.5 billion years ago
after an accumulation of dust and
debris lumped through
gravity
a solar system
one among countless others
in a great web
throughout emptiness of space
unending, all ten quarters
of the great void, inside the
womb of Tathagata.

The swollen river brooks no
banks
it glimmers down the
channel
a silver shimmer
carried on the
living water
swirling and
gurgling, a baby's
chatter
moving-on to the Father
of waters
Ocean
in the arms of
Mother, Gaia
born before the
swoon of
water
in infant time
when worlds' collided
out of sight
and mind.

Trickle

Shallow dried-up river
crawling through the
channel, late
September
two ducks swimming downstream
on tiny ripples; sounds of
car motors in the city, squeal
of brakes; squawk of
a crow on the
hillside, noise of a truck
beep beep beep
backing-up who knows where
or why, pale blue
sky floats on the
ripples
too.

Sunset #1

the sky lowers like a curtain
until it touches the ridge line
that darkens
as strobe lights
change the color of sky
blue to yellow to orange
to red, and
the sun sinks into
Ocean
and floats to the other side of
Earth
and rises
in the morning
pushed up by tides
influenced by
the ever-lovin'
Moon.

Ducks

I sat on the stone wall above the
green & gold river and
watched four ducks float down the
channel;
the sun glimmered on the
water and the
restless city murmured:
cars & trucks in endless procession.
The ducks preened atop a log
as yellow leaves on the
water moved like swimmers on the
ripples;
the
sun warmed my face,
my hands—
the ducks swam
down river.

Ditty

Dingy sky like a used dish rag
wrung-out over
streets and houses;
the ridge line stands up
for itself and
birds fly past the window
like darts;
on the ground a squirrel,
tail a waving flag:
gentlemen and
ladies, start your
engines!
The black eyes of the houses
do not blink:
roof top tuques with
chimney tassels—
the sound of distant traffic
makes me sleepy—
a bird glides in
like a musical note
and it and I
start to sing.

Leaves falling, clouds
moving-in, a cooler
wind than yesterday's;
a golden carpet to walk
on, burnished yellows
and browns; orange and
green (prettiest seen,
I think) blood red to
russet, orange to mustard
yellow; top masts above
the leaves, the trees will
be skeletons by Halloween.

Visitor

A wolf standing by
my bed:
I kick out at it and
wake
to the echo
of a shout in the
bedroom…
Too early to get up
but
I do
get up,
make coffee and
sit in my chair
by the window;
the sky blue & gray
like the Civil War—
puffs of cloud smoke
from cannons
and birds
lined-up
on the telephone wire
in formation.

Reprieve

the sun
at last
out from
behind a cloud
and the city
sparkles and glimmers
in chrome and glass
as shadows cross
sidewalks and
streets
whitened until
the sun goes back
behind the cloud
and the day
turns Winter-gray
again.

Flaming

from out of the
factory smokestack floats
a seahorse
that turns into an eagle
landing feet first
in baby blue
sky from
ridge line to ridge line
presided over by the
sun, a diamond
glinting,
corona of
cold flame.

Diary Entry #14

I fell asleep in my chair
today
while trying to read.
I blew phlegm out my nose
today
until my handkerchief sodden.
I slept in my car
today
while parked in the lot—
drifted-off as
chickadees played
hide & seek
in the hedge
across the street.

Periods

From the smokestack beside the
High School flows
semi-colons
one after another
their shadows glide across the
sidewalk and
full colons follow
until
the wind shifts
and India rises
from the stack
then fragments
into an archipelago of
islands, small as periods,
like the one
ends this
poem.

Those Crows Massed

in the trees
they croak my name
forlornly
born a human they crow
for shame!
You awe to be one
of us
croakers
like you was
one Springtime long ago
you do not remember, do you?
You croak your own tune
now, you being of
awe
awe!
Protuberance is the name
we caw you
caw you
caw!

Closure

the river no bigger
than a creek, softly
purling, slowly closing
for the season—you know
the reason—reopening in
March or May, depending
upon what the gods say
about the temperature
and duration of Winter.

www.ingramcontent.com/pod-product-compliance
Lightning Source LLC
LaVergne TN
LVHW041441170726
843492LV00008B/2741